Lennox

by Iain Gray

WRITING *to* REMEMBER

79 Main Street, Newtongrange,
Midlothian EH22 4NA
Tel: 0131 344 0414   Fax: 0845 075 6085
E-mail: info@lang-syne.co.uk
www.langsyneshop.co.uk

Design by Dorothy Meikle
Printed by Printwell Ltd
© Lang Syne Publishers Ltd 2021

All rights reserved. No part of this publication may be reproduced, stored
or introduced into a retrieval system, or transmitted in any form or by any
means (electronic, mechanical, photocopying, recording or otherwise) without
the prior written permission of Lang Syne Publishers Ltd.

ISBN 978-1-85217-771-3

Lennox

MOTTO:
I'll defend

CREST:
Two broadswords behind a swan's head

TERRITORY:
Vale of Leven, Dunbartonshire

NAME variations include:
Lenox,
Levenax

Chapter one:

The origins of the clan system

by Rennie McOwan

The original Scottish clans of the Highlands and the great families of the Lowlands and Borders were gatherings of families, relatives, allies and neighbours for mutual protection against rivals or invaders.

Scotland experienced invasion from the Vikings, the Romans and English armies from the south. The Norman invasion of what is now England also had an influence on land-holding in Scotland. Some of these invaders stayed on and in time became 'Scottish'.

The word clan derives from the Gaelic language term 'clann', meaning children, and it was first used many centuries ago as communities were formed around tribal lands in glens and mountain fastnesses.

The format of clans changed over the centuries, but at its best the chief and his family held the land on behalf of all, like trustees, and the ordinary clansmen and women believed they had a blood relationship with the founder of their clan.

There were two way duties and obligations. An inadequate chief could be deposed and replaced by someone of greater ability.

Clan people had an immense pride in race. Their relationship with the chief was like adult children to a father and they had a real dignity.

The concept of clanship is very old and a more feudal notion of authority gradually crept in.

Pictland, for instance, was divided into seven principalities ruled by feudal leaders who were the strongest and most charismatic leaders of their particular groups.

By the sixth century the 'British' kingdoms of Strathclyde, Lothian and Celtic Dalriada (Argyll) had emerged and Scotland, as one nation, began to take shape in the time of King Kenneth MacAlpin.

Some chiefs claimed descent from ancient kings which may not have been accurate in every case.

By the twelfth and thirteenth centuries the clans and families were more strongly brought under the central control of Scottish monarchs.

Lands were awarded and administered more and more under royal favour, yet the power of the area clan chiefs was still very great.

The long wars to ensure Scotland's

independence against the expansionist ideas of English monarchs extended the influence of some clans and reduced the lands of others.

Those who supported Scotland's greatest king, Robert the Bruce, were awarded the territories of the families who had opposed his claim to the Scottish throne.

In the Scottish Borders country – the notorious Debatable Lands – the great families built up a ferocious reputation for providing warlike men accustomed to raiding into England and occasionally fighting one another.

Chiefs had the power to dispense justice and to confiscate lands and clan warfare produced a society where martial virtues – courage, hardiness, tenacity – were greatly admired.

Gradually the relationship between the clans and the Crown became strained as Scottish monarchs became more orientated to life in the Lowlands and, on occasion, towards England.

The Highland clans spoke a different language, Gaelic, whereas the language of Lowland Scotland and the court was Scots and in more modern times, English.

Highlanders dressed differently, had different

customs, and their wild mountain land sometimes seemed almost foreign to people living in the Lowlands.

It must be emphasised that Gaelic culture was very rich and story-telling, poetry, piping, the clarsach (harp) and other music all flourished and were greatly respected.

Highland culture was different from other parts of Scotland but it was not inferior or less sophisticated.

Central Government, whether in London or Edinburgh, sometimes saw the Gaelic clans as a challenge to their authority and some sent expeditions into the Highlands and west to crush the power of the Lords of the Isles.

Nevertheless, when the eighteenth century Jacobite Risings came along the cause of the Stuarts was mainly supported by Highland clans.

The word Jacobite comes from the Latin for James – Jacobus. The Jacobites wanted to restore the exiled Stuarts to the throne of Britain.

The monarchies of Scotland and England became one in 1603 when King James VI of Scotland (1st of England) gained the English throne after Queen Elizabeth died.

The origins of the clan system

The Union of Parliaments of Scotland and England, the Treaty of Union, took place in 1707.

Some Highland clans, of course, and Lowland families opposed the Jacobites and supported the incoming Hanoverians.

After the Jacobite cause finally went down at Culloden in 1746 a kind of ethnic cleansing took place. The power of the chiefs was curtailed. Tartan and the pipes were banned in law.

Many emigrated, some because they wanted to, some because they were evicted by force. In addition, many Highlanders left for the cities of the south to seek work.

Many of the clan lands became home to sheep and deer shooting estates.

But the warlike traditions of the clans and the great Lowland and Border families lived on, with their descendants fighting bravely for freedom in two world wars.

Remember the men from whence you came, says the Gaelic proverb, and to that could be added the role of many heroic women.

The spirit of the clan, of having roots, whether Highland or Lowland, means much to thousands of people.

Meanwhile, many families proudly boast the heraldic device known as a Coat of Arms,.

The central motif of the Coat of Arms would originally have been what was sometimes borne on the shield of a warrior to distinguish himself from others on the battlefield.

Clan warfare produced a society where courage and tenacity were greatly admired

Chapter two:

'Not for glory nor riches...'

A locational surname, 'Lennox' derives from the Gaelic *leamhn* and in this case denoting 'the smooth stream' of the River Leven, and with *leamhnachd* indicating 'the field of the small stream.'

Anglicised as 'Levenauchen' or 'Levenachs' and then 'Levenax or Lennax', and further Anglicised through time as 'Lennox', this original 'field of the small stream' came to identify territory including the Vale of Leven in the present-day Scottish local authority area of Dunbartonshire.

A vast area, this territory from which those who came to dominate would take 'Lennox' as their surname, comprised present-day parishes and towns including Campsie, Kilsyth, Arrochar, Luss, Cardross, Drymen, Fintry, Dunblane, Dumbarton and, of course, Lennoxtown.

But what were the origins of those who would come to adopt the Lennox name?

Intriguingly, there are a number of possible

sources – one from an ancient Brittonic, or British, kingdom and another from those Anglo-Normans who acquired lands and territories north of the border.

What became the Lennox heartland was from the fifth century to approximately 1030 one of the core territories of the Brittonic Kingdom of Strathclyde, known in the Cumbric tongue as *Teyrna Ystrad Clut*.

Known by the Welsh as *Hen Ogledd* – the Old North – this sprawling area embraced northern England and southern Scotland and was also known as *Alt Clut*, from a Brittonic term for the fortress of Dumbarton Rock, the kingdom's main powerbase.

Having developed during the post-Roman period, it was originally home to the Brythonic tribe the Damnonii and appears to have become known as 'Strathclyde' – the 'strath' or 'valley' of the (River) Clyde – when its centre of power shifted to what is now the Govan area of Glasgow following the sacking of Dumbarton Rock by the Vikings in 870.

The gene pool of those who would later adopt the Lennox name was added to by those Normans who fought with William the Conqueror at the battle of Hastings in 1066 and also through Anglo-Normans who arrived after the conquest.

According to Lennox clan tradition, their forebears were Anglo-Saxons forced to quit their original territory in Northumbria in the late eleventh century.

This was in the aftermath of a vicious purge launched against them and fellow Anglo-Saxon aristocrats and Danish settlers by William the Conqueror.

Following his defeat of King Harold II, the last Anglo-Saxon king, William was declared king and the complete subjugation of his subjects followed, with those Normans who had fought on his behalf rewarded with lands.

But trouble brewed for William in the north of his new realm, where Anglo-Danish rebellions had been stirred by Edgar Atheling, claimant to what had been the kingdom of Wessex.

In what is known as The Harrying of the North, William's response was brutal – laying waste from 1069 to 1070 to the northern shires, including the city of York and replacing native aristocracy, such as those who would come to bear the Lennox name in Scotland, with Normans deemed to be more loyal.

In 1071, King Malcolm III of Scotland married Margaret, a sister of Edgar Atheling and therefore had an affinity with the dispossessed northerners – welcoming them to settle in his realm.

Among them was 'Arkil' or 'Arkyll', who settled in Lennox – and it was one of his descendants, Ailín I of Lennox, also known as 'Alwin' or 'Alún', who came to rule the territory as Mormaer – a Celtic aristocratic rank equivalent to 'Earl' – of Lennox for a period approximately dated to sometime before 1178.

But it was not until the bitter and bloody Wars of Scottish Independence that the Earls of Lennox – having by now dropped the title 'Mormaer' in favour of 'Earl', marched in all their martial glory onto the pages of the nation's turbulent history.

To find the root cause of the wars, we have to travel back through the dim mists of time to 1290 when, following the death of the young Margaret, Maid of Norway and heiress to King Alexander III of Scotland, John Balliol and Robert Bruce, 5th Lord of Annandale became competitors for the crown.

There were several other competitors, in what became known as the Great Cause, but their claims were the strongest, and among the supporters of Bruce, known to history as Bruce the Competitor and grandfather of the future King Robert the Bruce, was Malcolm I, Earl of Lennox.

The Scottish nobility had asked King Edward I of England to arbitrate in the matter of the succession and, through his powerful influence, Balliol was pronounced the rightful heir and duly inaugurated as such in November of 1292.

But the ambitious and haughty Edward declared himself Lord Paramount of Scotland and Balliol was accordingly treated as a mere vassal, owing fealty to the English monarch.

Deeply rankled by this humiliating state of affairs, a number of Scottish nobles concluded an alliance with France, the Auld Alliance, in July of 1295, and Edward's response was to invade the northern kingdom.

As his forces wreaked fire and havoc across Scotland, Balliol was forced to abdicate in July of the following year and, on Edward's orders, the proud arms of Scotland were formally torn from his tunic – giving the hapless Balliol the nickname of 'Toom Tabard', or 'Empty Coat.'

Imprisoned for a time in the Tower of London, he was later allowed to retire to his French estates in Picardy, where he died in 1314.

The Scots rose in revolt against the imperialist designs of Edward in July of 1296 but, known as 'the Hammer of the Scots', he brought the entire nation under his subjugation little less than a month later, garrisoning strategic locations throughout the length and breadth of the nation, and demanding the signing of a humiliating treaty of fealty.

Reluctantly signed at Berwick by 1,500 Scottish earls, bishops and burgesses, the parchment is known as the *Ragman Roll* because of the profusion of ribbons that dangle from the seals of the signatories – among whom were the Bruces and Malcolm I of Lennox.

But subjugation under the iron fist of English occupation did not sit well with the proud Scots, and the great patriot William Wallace raised the banner of revolt in May of 1297.

A charismatic leader and an expert in the tactics of guerrilla warfare, he and his hardened band of freedom fighters who included Malcolm I of Lennox and his kinsfolk, set Scotland aflame – boosting the morale of their fellow countrymen as they inflicted a stunning series of defeats on the English garrisons.

This culminated in the liberation of practically all of Scotland following the battle of Stirling Bridge, on September 11, 1297.

But, defeated at the battle of Falkirk on July 22, 1298, after earlier being appointed Guardian of Scotland, Wallace was eventually betrayed and captured seven years later, and brutally executed in London as a 'traitor' on August 23, 1305.

His execution only served to further inflame Scottish passions, and the cause of the nation's freedom was taken up again, this time under the inspired leadership of Robert the Bruce – grandson of Robert Bruce, 5th Lord of Annandale – who had been enthroned as king at Scone in March of 1306.

Meanwhile, Malcolm I of Lennox had died in 1303 and was succeeded by his son Malcolm II of Lennox – who rallied to the Bruce cause, attending his enthronement.

Over the next six years, Bruce experienced defeats but also stunning success that culminated in his great victory over the King Edward II at the battle of Bannockburn in midsummer of 1314.

While his father Malcolm I of Lennox had been one of the reluctant signatories in 1297 to the humiliating treaty of fealty the *Ragman Roll*, Malcolm II was one of the signatories to a much more proudly memorable document whose sentiments continue to resonate throughout the ages.

This is the famous *Declaration of Arbroath*, dated April 6, 1320 and addressed to Pope John XXII.

Signed by 31 barons and eight earls including

Malcolm II of Lennox and believed to have been written in Arbroath Abbey by Bernard of Kilwinning, Chancellor of Scotland and Abbot of Arbroath, it asserts the nation's right to independence and determination to resist subjugation by the English.

The original letter sent to the pope has long since been lost, but a surviving copy is held by the National Archives of Scotland, part of the National Records of Scotland.

Placed in 2016 on the UK Memory of the World Register, part of UNESCO's Memory of the World Programme and marking its 700th anniversary in 2020, one stirring passage reads:

..for, as long as but a hundred of us remain alive, never will we on any conditions be brought under English rule. It is in truth not for glory, nor riches, nor honours that we are fighting, but for freedom – for that alone, which no honest man gives up but with life itself

Chapter three:

High honours and distinction

A patriot to the last, Malcolm II of Lennox was killed for the cause in 1333 at the battle of Halidon Hill.

The great warrior king Robert the Bruce had died in 1329 and was succeeded by the five-year-old King David II.

Eager to take advantage of a dispute among the Scottish nobles over the young king's succession, an ambitious King Edward III of England gave his support to David's rival Edward Balliol, confident he could use him as a mere puppet for his own imperialist aims.

A mighty English force invaded Scotland in August of 1332, defeating the Scots in battle at Dupplin Moor, near Perth. Balliol was enthroned as King of Scots at Scone the following month and, as Edward had plotted, swore fealty to him.

Nationalist passions were aroused, however, and Andrew Murray, who had been appointed

Guardian of Scotland, raised the banner of revolt against the puppet Scots king and sent him fleeing across the border.

But in May of 1333 Edward returned with another army, laid siege to Berwick Castle, and met the Scots in battle at Halidon Hill, to the northwest of Berwick, on July 19.

Murray had already been captured and the new Guardian was Archibald, Lord of Douglas, who arranged his forces in three tightly packed groups of spearmen known as schiltrons, and a division of 1,200 knights.

They proved no match, however, for the deadly skill of the English archers and the knights who had taken better strategic advantage of the terrain.

The English victory was so complete that while Douglas, Malcolm of Lennox, his fellow earls of Ross, Sutherland, and Carrick, 500 knights, seventy barons, and thousands of Scots foot soldiers were slain, the English were reported to have lost only a mere fraction.

Malcolm's son and heir, Domhnall, died in 1365 and the earldom passed through his daughter Margaret, Countess of Lennox, to her husband and cousin Walter of Faslane.

Confusing matters somewhat – a trait that has subsequently bedevilled attempts to untangle the complex ownership of the title and its number of 'recreations' when bestowed on particular families – Margaret and Walter 'resigned' the title to the Crown.

But it was later 're-granted' to their son Duncan, whose daughter Isabella, Countess of Lennox, married Murdoch Stewart, 2nd Duke of Albany in 1420.

Despite their power and prestige, the Lennoxes fell victim to the vengeance of King James I in 1425 for their role – through their Albany connection – in the mysterious circumstances surrounding the death 23 years earlier of the king's older brother David, Duke of Rothesay, then heir apparent to the throne.

He died while being held in captivity by Robert, Duke of Albany and the king – having been held in captivity himself for a time in the English royal court – finally exacted a bloody vengeance when he returned to Scotland.

Isabella's father, husband and two of her sons were all executed.

No punitive action was taken against Isabella – perhaps it was thought she had suffered enough –

and she was allowed to return to Lennox Castle, her seat on the island of Inchmurrin, on Loch Lomond, where she died in 1458.

The Earl of Lennox title subsequently passed through a number of other aristocratic families, including the Stewarts of Darnley, with John Stewart, Lord Darnley, assuming the 're-created' title as 1st Earl of Lennox.

His son Matthew, 2nd Earl of Lennox, was among the 5,000 Scots including James IV, an archbishop, two bishops, eleven earls, fifteen barons, and 300 knights killed at the battle of Flodden in 1513.

The Scottish monarch had embarked on the venture after Queen Anne of France, under the terms of the Auld Alliance between Scotland and her nation, appealed to him to 'break a lance' on her behalf and act as her chosen knight.

Crossing the border into England at the head of a 25,000-strong army that included 7,500 clansmen and their kinsmen, James engaged a 20,000-strong force commanded by the Earl of Surrey.

Despite their numerical superiority and bravery, however, the Scots proved no match for the skilled English artillery and superior military tactics of Surrey.

The last of the Stewarts of Darnley to hold the Lennox title was Henry, Lord Darnley, the husband of Mary, Queen of Scots and who was murdered in a plot in 1567.

The title now passed to their son King James VI (James I of England), then to his uncle Charles Stuart and then, as a gift from the young monarch, to his close friend the French-born Esmé Stewart, who in 1581 was also created Duke of Lennox.

The glittering profusion of titles associated with the Earldom of Lennox was added to when Charles Lennox, the illegitimate son of King Charles II was granted the title 1st Duke of Richmond in addition to 1st Duke of Lennox and 2nd Duke of Aubigny.

The latter title came through his mother, the king's French-born mistress Louise de Kérouaille who was granted the title Duc d' Aubigny by King Louis XIV.

The first duke died in 1723 and his son, also Charles, born in 1701, inherited his titles.

An early patron on the game of cricket and instrumental in the first codification of the Laws of Cricket in 1744, he died in 1750, while through his wife Sarah Lennox (née Cadogan), he was the father of twelve children.

Among them were the four sisters known collectively to posterity as 'The Lennox Sisters' – Georgiana Fox, 1st Baroness Holland, Emily Fitzgerald, Duchess of Leinster, Lady Louisa Conolly and Lady Sarah Lennox.

Lady Sarah, born in 1745, led a particularly colourful life, including becoming a favourite for a time at court of King George III.

Having had a number of affairs and two failed marriages, she died in 1826, while a television mini-series *Aristocrats*, based on the lives of the sisters, was screened in 1999 – with Sarah portrayed by the actress Jodhi May.

In the present day, Charles Henry Gordon-Lennox, born in 1955 and owner of the Goodwood Estate in West Sussex, now holds the highly impressive titles of 11th Duke of Richmond, 11th Duke of Lennox, 11th Duke of Aubigny and 6th Duke of Gordon.

Going back to the nineteenth century, this was when the Lennoxes of Woodhead, a branch of Clan Lennox, were officially recognised as "chiefs of the family name of Lennox."

Their seat was Lennox Castle, a baronial mansion overlooking the Campsie Fells and about 1.5 miles (2.5km) from Lennoxtown, East Dunbartonshire.

Built between 1837 and 1841 for John Lennox Kincaid, it was sold to the former Glasgow Corporation along with its 1,222 acres of ground in 1927 and, with the addition of new buildings on the site, served as a hospital for mentally ill patients until 2002.

Excepting the actual castle itself, now A-listed, all the hospital buildings were demolished, while part of the site is now home to Celtic Football Club's Lennoxtown Training Ground.

Following the sale of the castle in 1927, the seat of the Lennoxes of Woodhead became for a time Downton Castle, near Ludlow, Shropshire, sold to a Greek owner in 1979.

The clan's proud heritage and traditions are still celebrated to this day through 'Clan Lennox', officially instituted as a society in 2017 and with the chief known as "Lennox of that Ilk and Woodhead, Chief of the Name and Arms of Lennox".

Chapter four:

On the world stage

Born in Aberdeen in 1954, Annie Lennox is the multi award-winning Scottish singer, songwriter and political activist who first rose to fame as a member of the bands The Tourists and Eurythmics and who now enjoys an equally successful solo career.

Her maternal grandmother and grandfather, she learned through the BBC's *Who Do You Think You Are?* television series in 2012, both worked at the Balmoral Estate on Royal Deeside – her grandmother as a dairy maid and her grandfather as a gamekeeper.

A more contemporary royal connection, however, had been made a year earlier when she was appointed an OBE by the Queen for her "tireless charity campaigns and championing of humanitarian causes."

Winning a place in the 1970s at the Royal Academy of Music, London, where she studied piano, harpsichord and flute, she later played the latter instrument with the band Dragon's Playground before collaborating with Dave Stewart in The Tourists and then the duo Eurythmics.

Top Eurythmics' hits throughout the 1980s include *Sweet Dreams (Are Made of This)*, *Here Comes the Rain Again*, *Who's That Girl?* and *Don't Ask Me Why*, while she also became noted for her androgynous look that saw her on stage wearing a man's business suit and with cropped, orange hair.

Named by *Rolling Stone* magazine as 'One of the 100 Greatest Singers of All Time', her solo hits include *Why* and *Walking on Broken Glass*, while she was also the recipient of both a Golden Globe Award and the 2004 Academy Award for Best Original Song for *Into the West*, soundtrack for the film *Lord of the Rings: Return of the King*.

Also the recipient to date of four Grammy Awards, an MTV Video Music Award and *Billboard* magazine's Billboard Century Award, as a political activist she has supported causes including LGBT rights and awareness of how HIV/AIDS impacts on women and children in Africa.

Through her second marriage to the Israeli record producer Uri Fruchtmann, she is the mother of the singer, songwriter and model **Lola Lennox**, born in 1990, and the model and actress **Tali Lennox**, born in 1993.

A co-founder of the experimental pop band Animal Collective, **Noah Lennox** is the American singer, songwriter and musician better known as **Panda Bear**.

Born in 1978 in Baltimore, Maryland and adopting 'Panda Bear' as a nickname through his habit of drawing pictures of the animal for the artwork of his recordings, in addition to his work with Animal Collective as a solo artist his albums include the 2007 *Pitch Perfect*.

From music to film, **Michael Lennox** is the award-winning Northern Irish director from Co. Antrim.

Debuting with his 2008 short film *Rip and the Preacher*, two years later he directed *Eclipse*, an episode of the BBC drama series *Coming Up*, while his short film *Boogaloo and Graham* won a BAFTA Award for Best Short Film and was nominated for the Academy Award for Best Short Film, Live Action.

Bearers of the Lennox name have also excelled in the highly competitive world of sport.

Nicknamed 'Buzz Bomb' by his fans because of his speed on the pitch, **Bobby Lennox** is the

Scottish former football winger and Celtic legend born in 1943 in Saltcoats, Ayrshire.

Signed for Celtic when aged 18, he went on to score 301 goals for the club, while also earning ten international caps – including scoring one of the goals in Scotland's memorable defeat of England at Wembley in 1967, the team's first defeat since winning the World Cup.

For Celtic, he was part of the team – now known to posterity as the Lisbon Lions – that won the 1967 European Cup after defeating Inter-Milan in the Estádio Nacional Stadium in Lisbon, Portugal.

Also known as 'Lemon' because of his ability to make defenders look like 'suckers', he played for a time in the United States with Houston Hurricane before returning to Celtic in 1978 and later joining its coaching staff

The recipient of an MBE and an inductee of the Scottish Football Hall of Fame, his autobiography *A Million Miles for Celtic* was published in 1982.

On American shores and in the much different sport of basketball, **Betty Lennox** is the American former player whose nicknames include 'Betty Basketball' and 'Betty Big Buckets.'

Born in 1976 in Oklahoma City, she played

in the Women's National Basketball Association (WNBA) for teams including Tulsa Shock, Minnesota Lynx, Seattle Storm and Los Angeles Sparks.

Two bearers of the Lennox name who have left enduring marks on the landscape are the bridge-builder David Lennox and the architect Edward Lennox.

Born in Ayr in 1788, **David Lennox** was the Scots-Australian master mason and bridge-builder who immigrated to Australia when aged 44, following the death of his wife.

Settling firstly in New South Wales, his skill as a stonemason was much in demand, and he was appointed Superintendent of Bridges, responsible for the maintenance of existing ones and the construction of new ones – including Lennox Bridge at Lapstone Hill, the oldest bridge on the Australian mainland.

Also responsible for the construction of a number of other bridges throughout Australia, including the second Prince's Bridge over the Yara River, Melbourne, he died in 1873.

In North America, **Edward Lennox**, born in 1854, was the Canadian architect responsible for more than seventy of Toronto's most notable structures designed in the late nineteenth and early twentieth centuries.

The son of Irish immigrants, he established his architectural firm in 1881 after studying at the Mechanics' Institute – progressing to design structures including Casa Loma and the Romanesque-Revival style neighbourhood The Annex.

He died in 1933, while his caricature – complete with handlebar moustache – is carved on the façade of his Old City Hall.

Still on North American shores, **David Lennox**, born in Detroit in 1855, was the American inventor and businessman whose legacy survives to this day through the global corporation Lennox International.

Specialising in heating, commercial refrigeration and air conditioning, the origins of the company go back to 1895 when Lennox helped to develop the first riveted-steel furnace.

Founding what later became the Lennox Furnace Company, he died in 1947.

One colourful but ultimately tragic bearer of the Lennox name was the Scottish poet and novelist **Charlotte Lennox** (née Ramsay).

Born in about 1730 in Gibraltar, she was the

daughter of James Ramsay of Dalhousie, a Scottish captain in the British Army, while her mother was of Scots-Irish roots.

Living for a time in New York after her father was posted to what was then the British colony of America, she eventually settled in London where she became friends with the great man of letters Samuel Johnson and the artist Joshua Reynolds – with Johnson becoming a leading admirer of her literary work.

This includes her 1750 *Harriet Stuart* and the 1790 *Euphemia*, but her most celebrated work is her *The Female Quixote*, or, *The Adventurers of Arabella*.

Published anonymously in 1752 and later translated into a number of other languages and an inspiration for Jane Austen's *Northanger Abbey*, the novel is a parody of Miguel de Cervantes' *Don Quixote* – where his romantic knight becomes the romantic female character Arabella.

Also author of the collection *Poems on Several Occasions* and taking to the stage as an actress for a time, she married Alexander Lennox who, despite his relative obscurity, claimed to be the rightful heir to the Earldom of Lennox – but the claim was rejected by the House of Lords on the basis of illegitimacy.

He and his wife had two children but became estranged, with Charlotte latterly reliant on financial support from the Literary Fund – living in 'solitary penury' until her death in 1804 and burial in an unmarked grave.